Rsell Harnard

Letters to Uncle Albert

Letters to Uncle Albert

with replies from Russell Stannard

faber and faber

LONDON · BOSTON

First published in 1996
by Faber and Faber Limited
3 Queen Square London WC1N 3AU

Printed in England by Clays Ltd, St Ives plc

© Russell Stannard, 1996

Russell Stannard is hereby identified as author of this
work in accordance with Section 77 of the Copyright,
Designs and Patents Act 1988

A CIP record for this book
is available from the British Library

ISBN 0–571–17508–2

10 9 8 7 6 5 4 3 2 1

Contents

Acknowledgements vi
Foreword vii

Atoms 1
The Sun 7
Planets 23
The Earth, Volcanoes and Earthquakes 35
The Moon 61
Stars 69
The Beginning of the World 89
The End of the World 105
God 111
Flying 125
Mind and Dreams 131
Growing Up and Getting Old 147
Lucky Dip 155
Fobbing Off! 165
Just Before I Go ... 170
The Children 171

Acknowledgements

Thanks from Uncle Albert and myself to all the children who have written to us asking questions.

I am especially grateful to the children of Barlby Primary School, London; Churchill Gardens School, London; St Peter's School, Earley, Reading; Harnham Junior School, Salisbury; Moira House School, Eastbourne; and Newlands Pre-Prep School, Eastbourne, for providing questions and for allowing me to try out my answers on them.

And, as always, thanks to my wife Maggi. She helped collect children's drawings, and put up with me every time I came to her waving another letter, exclaiming 'Hey, listen to *this* one!'

Foreword

When I began writing the Uncle Albert books, explaining to young people the science of Albert Einstein, I was surprised to get letters from readers – mostly addressed to Uncle Albert himself.

Many of the letters contained questions. These covered just about every subject under the Sun – scientific and non-scientific alike. This little book contains a first selection from them.

I have tried my best to answer the questions – on behalf of Uncle Albert. But some of them are so deep, neither I nor anyone else has an answer to them yet. Indeed, some of the questions are likely to remain for all time beyond any kind of answer.

So, the real interest of this book lies, not in my answers, but in the questions being asked. It's about time adults like myself recognized that young children think more deeply about things than we imagine. Indeed, I suspect they often think more deeply about them than we do ourselves.

Atoms

please can you tell
me: what is an atoms
made of

Lin age 8

my teacher
mr Lee.

Everything is made of atoms.

Take a grapefruit. You cut it in half. Next you cut each half into halves. Then you cut the halves of halves into halves, and you imagine doing this cutting, say, another 27 times. What do you end up with? A very, very tiny piece of grapefruit not worth eating? No. You end up with atoms. (I say 'imagine' doing this because you would need a *very* sharp knife to do it – and they don't come that sharp – and if they did, they would be dangerous, and you shouldn't be playing with it anyway.)

Atoms are the building blocks out of which the world is made. Animals, dirt, houses, foot-balls, clothes, the chair you are sitting on, this page you are reading – they are all made out of atoms stuck together.

I like to think of the world as a gigantic Legoland! When you take a model Lego car to pieces you don't end up with a smaller car; you end up with separate blocks – blocks with studs and holes. The more expensive the Lego set, the more different kinds of blocks you get. Some blocks are tiny – they have only one stud; others are a bit bigger with two studs, yet others have four studs, six etc. The world is made up from a 'Lego set' with 92 different kinds of building block, or atom.

The word 'atom' means 'something that cannot

be cut'. So, is that *it* – you can't cut an atom in half?

That's what people used to think. But now we know that isn't true. When you take an atom to pieces, you find, at the very centre, a tiny ball. It is called the 'nucleus' of the atom. And surrounding the nucleus are even tinier balls called 'electrons'. They buzz around the nucleus like bees round a hive.

An atom is mostly empty space. If you were to imagine it blown up to the size of an airport, the nucleus would be no bigger than a golf ball on the runway. As for the electrons, they would be smaller than peas, whizzing round the outside of the airport. So, the next time your mum says you can't have a second helping of stodgy pudding, try telling her: 'But, Mum, Uncle Albert says it's mostly empty space.' (You never know, it *might* work.)

What makes the 92 atoms different from each other? Two things. Firstly, they have a different sized nucleus. Secondly, they have a different number of electrons. The lightest atom has only one electron (like the smallest Lego brick having only one stud); the next one up has two electrons, the next three; and so on … all the way up to the heaviest atom which has (you've guessed it) 92 electrons.

When atoms are put together, the electrons rearrange themselves around their nuclei so as to make the atoms stick – in the same way as the studs and holes in the Lego blocks fit into each other. And just as you can build all sorts of different things out of the same set of Lego blocks – a toy tractor, a ship, a house etc. – so everything in the world can be built out of the same 92 types of atom. You simply arrange the pieces differently. Clever, don't you think?!

The Sun

Manprit Gill (age 10)

I would like you to answer my question. it is how was the sun made? And is it all gas and fire?

Yours sincerely
Hal Jarrett.

8

Yes, you are quite right: the Sun is a great ball of fiery gas. Like everything else, it is made of atoms. Except you don't need 92 types to make a Sun; just two kinds will do. These are the lightest atoms; they are called hydrogen and helium.

What happened was that there was this huge cloud of hydrogen and helium gas floating in space. Everything in the Universe pulls on everything else with a force called 'gravity'. (At this very moment you are being pulled down into your seat by the gravity force of the Earth.) The same was true of the atoms that made up this cloud; each atom in the cloud pulled on every other atom. Atoms are not very heavy so their gravity force is very gentle. But over a long period of time this force slowly squashed the cloud smaller and smaller.

Ever had a flat tyre? You get the bicycle pump, and you pump air into the tyre. As you do that you are squashing air. And what happens? The pump gets warm. And the harder you pump, the hotter it becomes. This is because when you squash air, or any other gas, it heats up.

That is what happened to the cloud of gas in space. The smaller it got (because of gravity) the hotter it became. In the end it got so hot, it suddenly caught fire.

I like Space. I wonder if
I will buy your Book anyway
I dont if you will get this
one there goes How long has
the Sun been in Space hope you
get it Right. See you soon bye bye for
now lots of Love Jamie Oilk
                              age 9.

The Sun caught fire (it was 'born') about 4,600 million years ago – and the fire has been burning ever since.

How can we grasp what 4,600 million years is like? One way is to imagine collecting calendars (the sort that have a new page for each month). You start saving them way back when the Sun was born, and you buy one every year. If you did that, by now, the pile of old calendars would be 10,000 kilometres high! That's almost the distance from one side of the Earth to the other.

I am Paul Reilly and I'm writing from Barlby School. I'm 10 years of age. My topic in school is earth and space and light and reflections. Me and the class have been reading your book "the time and space of uncle Albert" and so far it has been good.

We have found out so far abouts the beams of light from the sun, tempratures of different planets and menthane helium hydrogen gases in planets.

I would be grateful if you would awnser my question? Please could you tell me where the sun gets its heat from? I leave school in September so I was wondering if you could come to see us before the summer holidays.

yours sincerely
paul

In the early days, the Sun warmed up by having its gas squashed down. But since it 'caught fire', it has got its heat another way – from the atomic nuclei. (Notice we say 'nuclei', not 'nucleuses'. It's not my fault; I didn't invent the language.) What happens is that the Sun gets so hot, everything jiggles about like crazy – so much so, the electrons get knocked out of their atoms. The electrons and nuclei go charging about like mad, here and there in all directions at once, banging into each other.

When nuclei of hydrogen and helium crash into each other, they sometimes stick together. When this happens, they give out energy in the form of heat and light.

Why do they give out energy? It's a bit like two people who start off living in separate houses. They each need to use gas and electricity to keep warm, heat the bathwater, and do their cooking. But if they decide to live together, they cut their fuel bills. They can sit in the same heated room instead of separate ones, watch the same TV set, cook both their meals in the same heated oven, and so on. That means there is now more gas and electricity (energy) that can be used in other ways.

The same is true of the nuclei. When they get together, they don't need as much energy as when they were separate. So when they bang together and stick, out comes the energy they no longer need. And that's the energy that keeps the Sun burning. Of course, nuclei are so tiny you wouldn't expect much to come out of two of them sticking together. But when you've got squillions upon squillions of them doing it at the same time, it all adds up.

I am very intrested in
outer space I have got a lot of
book's and these are my questions.
would the sun ever blow up?
why? and when?.

from Ahmad (10)

14

Good question. The Sun is, in fact, like a giant nuclear bomb. It gets its energy in exactly the same way as a nuclear bomb does – through nuclei sticking (or fusing) together. But the great thing about the Sun is that it is a bomb going off s ... l ... o ... w ... l ... y.

It is really quite amazing how the Sun manages to do this – how it is able to feed the hydrogen fuel into its fire at just the right rate to keep the fire burning at a steady rate.

Mind you, this cannot go on for ever. It's not that the Sun is in any danger of suddenly blowing up. But some time in the future, it will slowly start to swell up. When it does, the Sun will turn red and almost fill the whole of our sky. The surface of the Earth will become mega hot, and all life will be burned to a frazzle.

That's the bad news. The good news is that you and I, and our children, and grandchildren, and our great grandchildren, and great great etc. ... will all be dead and gone long before this happens! The Sun is due to stay more or less the same as it is for about another 5,000 million years. So you can't use 'the end of the world is coming' as an excuse for not doing next week's homework. Tough!

My name is John I have
a brother a mum and dad a dog
and I live in london.

Are topic is about earth and
space. We have been learning about the
different planets and what they look
like and what they are made of.
We are reading your book The time
and space of uncle albert. I think
it is the best book I've read this
year. My best part is when there
are talking about the time on earth
and in space.

There are some question I
want to ask you we are on earth and
earth is in space but how do we
get if space is black? How do the
planets spins on there own axis? How
do you know what the sun is made
of if you cant touch it?

We are inviting you to come to
our class and talk to us about
earth and space. If you could come
before the summer holidays because
we are going to secondary school.

Yours Sincerely
John.

You're right, we can't touch the Sun. So, we have to make use of the light we get from it.

When you heat up atoms in a laboratory, they give out coloured light. For example, heat up atoms of sodium and they shine with a bright yellow light. (This is the light you get from yellow sodium street lights.) If you heat up another type of atom, neon, you get the pinkish light of neon strip lights; and so on. Not only that, if the sodium atom is *cold* rather than hot, it will swallow up any yellow light that is shone on to it, and neon will swallow up pink. So each type of atom has its own special likes and dislikes when it comes to colours.

This special mix of colours becomes a kind of atomic fingerprint. In fact, you can turn all this into a detective game. If I heat up some unknown mixture of atoms, can you tell me what atoms I've got simply by looking at the colours given out? That is the kind of detective problem set by the Sun. Instead of just saying the Sun is a sort of yellowy white, and leaving it at that, you measure very, very carefully exactly what colours are being given out and getting swallowed up. And that's how scientists learn that the Sun has been formed mostly out of the two lightest types of gas: hydrogen and helium – and they don't have to burn their fingers finding out!

'My name is John and because you are a Professor could If you awnser my questions. If the world started off with one person how comes naw there are millons of people?. Why do people get freckles? How did the planets get theer names? and how does the sun hurt our eyes if its so far away?.

If you could awnser my questions I would be very happy.

Yours Faithfully

(Age 11) John Baldry

The Sun *is* a long way from us. If a space craft were to fly to the Sun from the Earth, and it went at the same speed as a jumbo jet, it would take 20 years to get there. It is the distance that makes the Sun look small.

But in fact it is big – so big, a million Earths could fit inside it. Because of the distance, the Sun's disc covers only a tiny fraction of the sky. We get heat from only that small part of our sky; that's why the Earth is nice and warm instead of baking hot.

But the *brightness* of the Sun's small disc is more or less the same as if the Sun were right up close to us – because it travels most of the way through empty space, and there is nothing to block its path to us. So, although the disc is small, it is ever so bright – dangerously bright. After all, you can burn holes in wood with the Sun's rays using a magnifying glass. (So, what do you think you would be doing to the back of your eye if you looked directly at the Sun through the lens that makes up the front part of your eye?!)

The most precious thing about living is the sun. If the sun goes away for ever there will be no warmth or light or heat and it will be cold and it will be wet. If the sun goes away can we bring it back some way?

If we could not bring it back then How could we bring heat light and warmth back?

If there was no light how would the plant trees and flower grow?
I hope the sun does not go away. Come and visit my class at Barlby school and come and talk to us
you sincerely
David

As you say, the Sun is precious. Without its warmth, there would be no life on the Earth.

In olden days, people got very worried that the Sun might go away and not come back. After all, every evening at sunset it would disappear, and no one knew where it went to at night. Who could be sure it would be back next day? Even more alarming were eclipses. These happen when the Moon comes between us and the Sun, and so blocks out the Sun's rays for a short while. Fancy the Sun disappearing in the middle of the day without warning!

Nowadays we don't have to worry about such things. We know why the Sun sets and rises. We also understand why eclipses happen, and we can predict exactly when to expect them.

But *could* the Sun and Earth ever get separated? Not really. We now know that the Earth goes round the Sun in orbit. What stops it flying off into space? The force of gravity between them. If you try escaping from the Earth by jumping, the Earth's gravity pulls you back again. It is the same with the Earth and the Sun. Because the Sun is so massive, it has a huge gravity force, and it is this force that makes sure that the Earth will always stay close to it. And a good thing too!

Planets

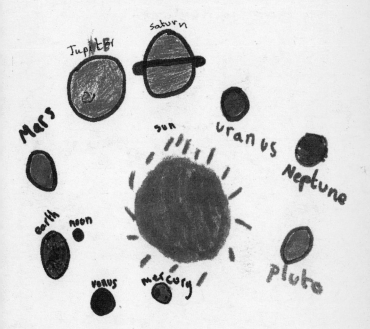

I am 6 years old.
I would like to know
about space. How many
planets are there in
space? love sarah xx

Nine of them. Starting closest to the Sun we have Mercury, Venus, Earth, Mars, Jupiter, Saturn, Uranus, Neptune and Pluto.

They all go round the Sun, each one in a bigger and bigger orbit. Earth goes round in one year – that's what we mean by a year. Pluto's year is the longest: 248 Earth-years. Mercury goes round in 88 days – a quarter of the time. So, if you are 10 years old, say, and someone was born on Mercury the same day as you, they would reckon themselves to be 40 by now – 40 *Mercury*-years old, that is. (Not that anyone ever does get born on Mercury – being so close to the Sun, it is far too hot.)

Please will you try to answer my question. It is why are all the planets all different sizes?

yours
Sincerely
Emma

They *are* very different in size. Jupiter is the biggest. Its diameter (the distance from a point on its surface to the point on the exact opposite side) is eleven times bigger than that of the Earth. Pluto, on the other hand, is the titchiest – less than one-fifth of the Earth's diameter.

Not that even Pluto is all that small. If you lived on Pluto and decided to walk right round it, it would still take you a year to get back to your starting point – even if you walked 12 hours every day. As for doing a walking tour of Jupiter, that would be a real marathon; it would take you your whole lifetime.

Actually, be warned. It is not a smart idea to try to walk on Jupiter at all. It has no surface to walk on! It is really nothing more than a great ball of gas – one that gets denser and thicker the deeper you sink down into it. The same is true of all the really big planets: Jupiter, Saturn, Uranus and Neptune.

But, although some planets are mostly gas, and the others are rocky, they were all formed in the same way. At the time gases and dust clouds collected together to form the Sun, little eddies or whirlpools, were set up outside the centre (like you sometimes get when the water is going down the bath plughole). Instead of getting sucked into the newly formed Sun itself, they stayed outside, going in orbit round the Sun. They each squashed down (because of gravity) to form the planets.

For the inner planets close to the Sun, the light gases were blown away by the hot wind coming from the Sun, leaving the collected dust which then formed the rocky planets. Further out, the planets like Jupiter were able to hold on to their light gases – that's why they are still mostly gas.

So, why are the planets different sizes? It depends on how much gas was originally captured into each whirlpool, and whether they were sufficiently far from the Sun to be able to hang on to their gas once the Sun caught fire and started blasting out its hot wind.

I have a question
for you perhaps you could answer for me
how far is marcury from the sun?
If you cun answer this question
Don't take to long witing back

from
Andrew
Buchanan

A

Although it is the closest of the planets to the Sun, it is still 58 million kilometres from the Sun.

How far is that? Imagine a length of string wrapped round the Earth's equator. Now stretch it out straight. It would take 14,500 such pieces of string, placed end to end, to reach from Mercury to the Sun (and 37,500 to reach from Earth to the Sun).

From the surface of Mercury, the Sun would look three times larger than it does from the Earth; that's why it is boiling hot there and no one would be able to survive living there.

could you please tell me
why pluto the coldest planet. Not the
hotest.

Thank you
(3R) From
Adam chandler

Having read my answer to the last letter that should be an easy one to answer now. Pluto is the furthest of the planets from the Sun. Outer space is very, very cold. To keep warm one must be close to a fire of some sort (like the Sun).

If, on a freezing winter night a cat called Mercury is curled up on a rug 30 centimetres from a gas fire (which we'll pretend is the Sun), and an Earthling is stretched out on the sofa one metre from the fire, then on that scale, the poor old dog, Pluto, would be shivering 40 metres down the road!

While I was watching a space programme with my sister they showed a map of space. I stared at saturn and thought why does saturn have rings?

Yours sincerely
Joseph Stewart.

As a boy, I lived for a year with my Uncle Bill. (It was during the Second World War, when it was too dangerous for children to live at home in London because of the bombing.) He had a wonderful telescope. It was his hobby. He loved looking at the stars through it, and showed me all sorts of wonderful things through it. It was Uncle Bill who first got me interested in 'what was up there'.

Several years later, when he became too old to go star-gazing on cold nights, he gave me his telescope. It is still my pride and joy.

Without doubt, the greatest thrill I ever had with my telescope was the sight of Saturn and its beautiful rings. So, what are they? They are very flat and thin. But they are not solid; they are not rigid. They are in fact made up of a vast number of pieces of ice. Some are like snowflakes, others like dirty snowballs, and some are as big as a snowman's body. They slowly move round and round the planet, much like the Moon goes round the Earth. In fact, you can think of these icy bits as very tiny moons.

We now know that Saturn is not alone in having rings. Jupiter, Neptune and Uranus also have some, but they are very thin and hard to see even when they are photographed from close up by a space probe.

The Earth, Volcanoes and Earthquakes

Everything has a begining, rubber comes from rubber trees which come from seeds from older trees and people come from their mothers and have a birth date like mine is the 29th of December. How was the earth made and when?

from
Kathryn Brown
age 9

With a birthday that close to Christmas, I bet you have problems getting people to remember it. I speak from experience; my birthday is Christmas Eve. I always insist on having my own birthday cake – not to be muddled up with the Christmas cake! Stick up for your rights, Kathryn!

As for your question, I have already pointed out that the Earth is a planet like the others. So, it was formed out of a whirlpool of gas and dust outside the Sun. We think it was formed at the same time as the Sun and the other planets, i.e. 4,600 million years ago.

How do we know that? Because of radioactivity (pronounced 'radio–activity', except that it has nothing to do with the activity of listening to Walkmans). What happens is that some very heavy atomic nuclei are too big and wobbly for their own good. After a while, bits get thrown off, or fall off them – leaving a somewhat smaller, more sensible-sized nucleus. When a nucleus slims down in this way, we say it has 'decayed'; it has radioactively decayed. For any particular type of nucleus half of them decay in a certain time called its 'half life'. For example, the half life might be one million years. That means, if you start off with 16 oversized nuclei, after one million years you will be left with half of them, namely eight. So that gives you eight nuclei that are still oversized, plus eight new sensible-sized nuclei. After *another* one million years, half of the remaining eight over-sized nuclei will also have decayed. That means that after a total of two million years, we shall have only four nuclei that are still oversized, and four more sensible-sized ones to add to the eight we already have, giving a total of 12 sensible-sized ones.

To begin with:
●●●●●●●●●●●●●●●●

After 1 million years:
●●●●●●●● ○○○○○○○○

After 2 million years:
●●●● ○○○○ ○○○○○○○○

Can you see how this gives us a way of working out how long a collection of nuclei has been around? Try the following quiz:

Question

Suppose I have a collection of nuclei like those we have just been talking about. In this collection, there are two oversized ones and 14 sensible-sized ones. Can you tell me how long my collection of nuclei has been around?

(DON'T READ THE NEXT PAGE TO LOOK AT THE ANSWER UNTIL YOU HAVE HAD A GO AT IT YOURSELF!)

Answer

If it took 2 million years to go from 16 oversized nuclei to four oversized and 12 sensible-sized nuclei, it will take another 1 million years for half of the remaining four to decay, so leaving two oversized ones and a total of 14 sensible-sized ones. So, a mixture of two oversized and 14 sensible-sized nuclei means it must have been around for a total of 3 million years. So that's the answer.

By examining the dirt of the Earth, and counting how many oversized nuclei we have compared to sensible-sized nuclei, we can work out how old the collection is. That is how scientists are able to work out that the Earth is 4,600 million years old. And because they believe the Sun was formed at the same time as the Earth, that must be how old the Sun is.

Here is a question
for your book. "If the sun is so
far away how come the middle
of the world is so hot? you would of
thought it would be cold" I hope you
can answer my question

Lots of love
melanie (age 10)

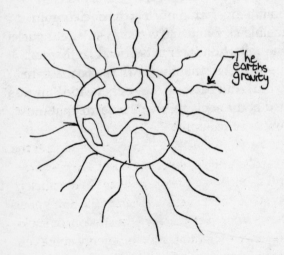

The
earths
gravity

Good point. You *would* expect it to be cold down there. After all, space is very cold. The reason the surface of the Earth is warm is that it gets heated up by the Sun during the day; at night it rapidly loses heat to space. I don't have to tell you how quickly things cool down in winter on a clear night once the Sun has set.

But in fact, if you go down a mine, the deeper you go, the *warmer* it becomes. As for the centre of the Earth, it is very, very hot – so hot, it melts rocks! And that is without it *ever* seeing the Sun down there. So, what's going on?

It's all to do with those atomic nuclei again. Remember how the Sun got its heat? Light nuclei banged into each other and fused together to form somewhat heavier nuclei. As they did this, some heat energy was given out. We said the Sun was a kind of nuclear bomb going off slowly.

Well, there is another kind of nuclear bomb. It's going off quietly *under our very feet*! Remember the big oversized nuclei throwing off bits to become more sensible-sized? Those changes to the nuclei also send out heat energy. Whereas the Sun's energy comes from nuclear *fusion* (the fusion, or sticking together, of light nuclei), the energy at the centre of the Earth comes from nuclear *fission* (the fission, or splitting up, of heavy nuclei).

But, Ah! you're thinking to yourself, he told Paul (p. 13) just now that you save energy when

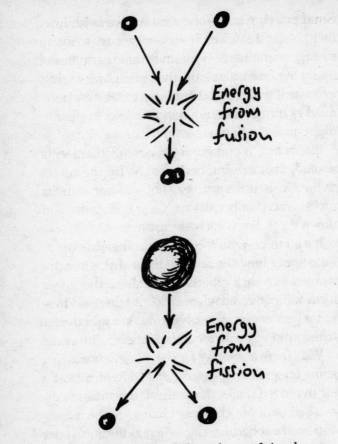

Energy from fusion

Energy from fission

you live together. That's how he explained energy from fusion. Now he is saying the *opposite* – that you save energy when you split up. He can't have it both ways.

Oh no? Who says? If you have a house with a

teenager living in it – one who is always leaving the lights and the TV on – it is very easy to save energy when they leave home! Some people save energy when they get together, others when they split up. The same goes for nuclei. Some nuclei give out energy through fusion; others by fission.

Of course, you don't get much energy out of just one nucleus splitting up. But as we saw with fusion, when you get lots and lots of nuclei all doing the same thing at the same time, it adds up.

What happens to all this energy being produced deep down in the Earth? It makes its way to the Earth's surface. From there it is able to escape into space. But this takes a long time; the heat has to travel thousands of kilometres to get to the surface. Because of this, the temperature builds up – to the point where it melts the rocks.

It's quite a thought that the solid-looking land we walk on is not actually solid all the way down. It is in fact just a thin crust floating on a hot liquid – a bit like the cool skin that forms on the surface of hot custard!

(Which reminds me: I *love* the skin on custard; do you? I always had the skin. But then I got married. To my horror I discovered that my wife's mother also loved the skin on custard. Can you imagine: two grown-ups fighting over who was to get the skin?!)

Could you please tell
what happens inside
rock befor an earthquak
Thank you
        from
          ThomasCompton

I have just told Melanie how the land is actually a thin crust floating on molten (or melted) rock. This liquid churns about because of all the heat that is coming from down below. The liquid rubs against the underside of the crust on top – and that makes the crust slide about. Cracks form in the crust, so it ends up as separate pieces called 'plates'. It's a bit like a jigsaw of broken dinner plates fitted together.

There is one of these cracks, for example, running down the west coast of the USA. The city of San Francisco is built mainly on one of these plates, and that of Los Angeles, about 600 kilometres south of San Francisco, is on the other side of the crack.

Interesting things happen near these cracks, or 'faults' as they are called. The churning liquid underneath one of the plates might be slowly moving that plate in one direction, while the liquid under the next-door plate is moving that one in a different direction. This is happening in California. Los Angeles is advancing towards San Francisco. Not that the rail fare between the two cities shows any signs of being reduced year by year. The gap is closing at the rate of only five centimetres per year. But if you're prepared to postpone your journey for 10 million years, by then the two cities will be opposite each other – and you'll be able to walk across!

But what, you ask, has this to do with earth-quakes? It's all right; I haven't forgotten the question. It's just that sometimes the answer takes a while coming. Here it is:

If we had a giant oil-can, we could keep the gap between two plates nicely oiled all the time, so the two could slide smoothly past each other. That way all would be well; there would be no earthquakes. But it is not like that. For much of the time the plates get caught up and stuck together at the boundary between them. While the main parts of the two plates continue to move past each other at a steady rate of a few centimetres per year, the edges aren't budging at all; they are being left behind. After 10 or 20 years of this, they might be lagging by a metre. Strains are set up in the rocks on either side of the divide. Another 10 or 20 years, and they are now lagging by a couple of metres. The strains are increasing. Another 10 years … It can't go on like this. It is like trying to stretch a rubber band. You can go just so far, then …

TWANG!

The twang is the earthquake. A point is reached where the strains are so great that the rocks split, the plates free themselves from each other, and suddenly jerk forwards in the direction they have been trying to go in. There is a shudder that ripples outwards from the fault causing damage to buildings. Often people get killed.

What happens then? The plates get caught up again, and the whole thing is set to repeat itself once more. There is then another earthquake – near the same place – in a few years' time. Then another, and another …

If it is known that some places, like California, are dangerous (San Francisco was completely destroyed by an earthquake in 1906), why do people live there, you might ask? Why not be sensible and go and live in the middle of a plate where there is little chance of an earthquake? Good idea. I used to think people who lived in California must be thick or something. But then, when I was a young scientist, I got the offer of a very interesting job. It was at the world's leading place for doing my type of nuclear physics. The trouble was it was right next to San Francisco! What should I do?! (What would *you* have done?) I thought about it – and decided to go. I stayed there a whole year. Does that mean I'm thick? Probably. Thick – but lucky; it was a wonderful year.

We are reading
"Black holes and uncle Albert" at
school. I have a question for you.
Why do Volcano's explode? I would
like to know this because i like the
volcano colours when they explode.

Yours sincerely
Miss Sarah
Bartholomew

Volcanoes occur where there is a weak spot in the Earth's crust. Over a period of time, pressure builds up in the molten rock down below. This goes on until the crust can no longer keep the lid on. Suddenly, the weak point gives way and the molten rock comes shooting out. That is how the explosion happens. As the molten stuff comes out, it cools down to form ash and solid rock, which then gets dumped all around the hole. Each time there is an eruption, the mound of ash and rock grows. In the end, there is so much of it, it becomes a mountain – a mountain with a hole at the top, where the stuff is still coming out.

These weak points often occur at the boundary between two plates. So what with earthquakes, and now volcanoes, it really is a good idea not to live in such places!

As you say, volcano explosions can be very beautiful – like a gigantic free firework display. But they are very dangerous and destructive. In 1883, a particularly large one occurred at Krakatoa, on an island in the Indian Ocean. It killed 40,000 people. The sound of the explosion could be heard 5,000 kilometres away.

At night when the sun goes down I wonder where it goes, does it go into the sea or does it go to Australia. Is it is not any of those tell me the answer any way.

yours sincerely
Elliot Wright
age: 9

For a long time everyone thought that the Earth was flat. Each morning the Sun would rise up, pass overhead, and then disappear into the distant ground, or sea, in the evening. As we saw earlier, when I was writing to David (p. 21), this was very worrying. What if the Sun decided not to come back again the next day?

But then it was discovered that the Earth was *not* flat. It was round, like a ball. As for the Sun, it journeyed in an orbit around the Earth. At night time it didn't dive into the sea; it simply went round and shone on a different part of the

Earth's surface, before reappearing the other side.

This certainly seemed to explain things nicely. Except that this idea was also wrong!

You know how when you sit on a roundabout in the park, it looks as though everything – the trees, the park benches, the prams – are all whizzing round you. But they're not really. It is not *they* who are moving, it is *you*; your roundabout is spinning. Well, that's how it is with the Earth. The Sun is *not* moving round us; it is the Earth that is spinning. It spins about a line (or 'axis') passing through the Earth from the North pole to the South pole.

Starting with the Sun directly overhead at noon, it takes 24 hours to complete a turn and have the Sun directly overhead again. That is what we mean by one 'day'.

All the planets spin, but at different rates. So their 'days' are different from ours. Jupiter's day is just under 10 hours; Mercury's is 176 Earth-days.

So, the answer to your question is that at night time the Sun goes to Australia – or better still, it is the turn of Australia to spin round to face the Sun.

I have a
question for you to try and
answer, does the world spin so
fast or so slow that we
don't notice it spinning?

Yours sincerely,

Naomi Durston.

HELP

spinning fast

HELP

You might wonder why it took so long for people to twig that the Earth was spinning like a roundabout. After all, if you ride a roundabout all day, you *know* it's you that is moving – you end up dizzy! So why don't people at the North and South poles end up dizzy? And why don't those living along the equator get flung off into space? You've guessed it. It's because the Earth spins so slowly. No one gets dizzy on a roundabout that takes a whole day to do one turn.

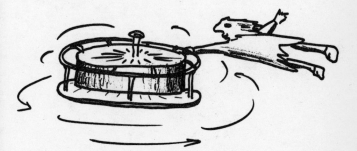

'I have a question to ask you. It is: If it takes a year for the World to go round the Sun why do We have leap years?

Yours sincerely

Sophie Fowler

A *year* is how long it takes the Earth to go right round the Sun in its orbit and get back to its starting point. A *day* is how long it takes for the Earth to spin on its axis between noon one day and noon the next. But there is nothing to say that the Earth has to spin on its axis an exact number of times while completing one orbit round the Sun.

In fact, the Earth's year is 365¼ days long. This means that, having started its orbit at a particular point in space on 1 January, after 365 days (what we normally call a 'year' – from 1 January to 31 December) the Earth is not quite back to where it was at the start. After two 'years' it is lagging by twice as much; after three 'years', three times as much. After four 'years' it would take the Earth four quarter-days to make up the difference. But four quarter-days are, of course, one whole day.

Which is where the neat trick comes in. Every fourth year we announce that there is an extra day to the 'year' – 366 instead of 365. During that extra day the Earth is able to catch up. By the next 1 January, it is ready to start the new 'year' from the proper starting point of its orbit. The extra day is tacked on to the end of February – to give 29 February. (Don't ask me why; I reckon it should have been 32 December.) Anyway, it's a good idea (provided that you don't have your birthday on 29 February). Without these leap years, as they are called, the calendar would gradually slip. Winter would eventually come round in July, and summer at Christmas time. (Which is something the Australians have always had to put up with; but that's their problem!)

PS Actually that's not the end of it. The Earth does not orbit the Sun in *exactly* 365¼ days – it's a little bit less than that. So, even after a leap year, the Earth isn't *quite* back to where it ought to be; it is now a teeny bit *ahead*. So to make up for this, every hundredth year (those ending in 00 like 1800 and 1900) have an ordinary 365-day year instead of having a 366-day leap year.

PPS Even that isn't the end of it. That skipping of a leap year every hundredth year, now leaves the Earth just a teeny weeny bit *behind* where it ought to be. So to make up for this, every *four hundreth* year (like the year 2000), instead of having an ordinary year, they have a leap year.

PPPS By now, I bet you're wishing you hadn't asked!

I have been wondering for ages and I would like to now, if I started digging in someones back garden or in my playground would I find gold? I have been wanting to know this because I think I have gone bankrupt. (Joke)
I'll be looking forward to seeing you.

yours sincerely
Mark currie
(Age 11.)

Digging up the playground? Think twice, Mark!

Gold is rare. It's only to be found in certain regions – like parts of South Africa and the USA. I don't recall anyone striking gold in a London back yard. Mind you, I have heard of young lads getting pocket money for digging a *garden*. Why not have a word with your mum or dad and see if you can't fix up some arrangement. Either that or get a paper round.

I was doing some gardening in my section of garden when my mum called me in, "And wash your filthy hands." she said. I looked down at my hands, they were brown! It set me wandering why soil wasn't red, yellow or blue. Do you know why? I wish it was skin colour, then I wouldn't have to wash my hands!

Yours sincerely,

Stephanie Orme (age 9)

one of my hands

Soil comes in many different colours. I'd say sandy soils were yellow, wouldn't you? As for red, I've seen red and pink rocks and hills in the USA, and in desert countries like Egypt and Jordan. In fact, I've seen dirt that was more or less the colour of skin. Mind you, it was in the middle of a baking hot desert called Death Valley. I wouldn't want to live there, even if I could get away without washing my hands at meal-time!

As for blue stones, there are some of those too. Not many. They are called sapphires and amethysts. They are so rare, if you are lucky enough to dig one up, you could sell it for a lot of money!

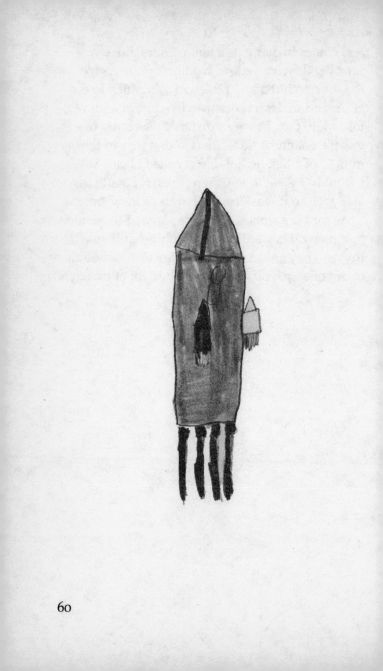

The Moon

When I went to bed and got to sleep I got up and looked out of my window. I looked at the moon then I wondered how was the moon made.

yours sincerely

Steven Jones Age 10

I have already described how the Sun and planets were made (p. 27). Remember how we started with a big swirling cloud of dust and gas? Most of it got drawn into the centre to form the Sun. But smaller eddies and whirlpools formed outside the centre. These settled down to become the planets going round the Sun.

One idea about how the Moon was born is that a very little whirlpool formed in the gas and dust outside the Earth. This squashed down and ended up as the Moon going round the Earth. That is certainly how we think the other planets got at least some of their moons (Pluto has one moon, like Earth, and Mars has two, but some of the bigger planets have lots: Neptune has eight, Uranus 15, Jupiter 16 and Saturn tops the league with *18*).

But that is not the only way to get a moon. In the early days, soon after the Sun and the nine planets formed, there were lots of rocks flying about. They were, if you like, very, very tiny planets. It is thought that some of them came too close to one of the big planets, and got captured in orbit about it. From then onwards they became one of the planet's moons.

But today most scientists think that *our* Moon wasn't formed in either of these ways. They think that, soon after the Earth formed, it was hit by one of these rocks flying through space. A huge chunk was knocked out of the Earth. This came out as a great 'splash' of molten rock. It went into orbit around the Earth, cooling and settling down to give us the Moon.

When we look at the Moon today, we see its surface pitted with craters formed when some more of those early rocks smashed into it.

could you please tell me
why is the moon white?

Thank you

From
Laura Bishop

The Moon isn't like the Sun; it doesn't give out any light of its own. So, how can we see it? By the light from the Sun reflecting from its surface. Sunlight is white, and the rocks on the Moon are a light greyish colour. The great flat plains, caused by molten rock bubbling up from down below and spreading out, are somewhat darker. That's why the Moon is blotchy and ends up looking like a face: 'The Man in the Moon'.

The phases of the Moon (whether it looks like a thin crescent, or a half Moon, or a full Moon) depend on the angle at which the Sun's light is striking the surface. It takes about a month for it to go through its full range of 'shapes', because that's how long it takes the Moon to complete its orbit around the Earth and get back to where it started.

On a clear night with a crescent Moon, if you look hard you can see the rest of the Moon making up the complete disc – the part that is in shadow from the Sun. How? By light coming from the Earth, and being reflected back to us by the darkened part of the Moon!

Earthlight is to a Moonling what moonlight is to an Earthling. Moonlings standing on the Moon at night time, see above their heads a shining Earth, lit by the Sun. So even though it's night time on that part of the Moon, the Moonlings can still find their way about with the help of faint earthlight. *PS Moonlings*!?! Since when have there been … ?

This is a question for your book. "If the moon comes out at day time, why dosen't the sun come out at night"?

Love
from

matthew Age 5

The Sun shines all the time. It gives out so much light it turns everything into day. When we talk about 'day time' we actually *mean* that time when the Sun is up. If ever the Sun decided to come up in the middle of the night (it can't – but just suppose it *did*), it would straight away shine its bright light on everything and turn night into day!

Not so the Moon. The Moon gives out only a faint light. If it comes up in the middle of the night, so what? It sheds its gentle moonlight, but that is not enough to turn night into day. As for the day time, it can come out, and again it doesn't make any difference – it's still just normal day time.

So, although the Sun is big and important and makes everything day time when it is around, I reckon the Moon has more fun. Like us, it can enjoy the evenings and the restful night times as well as the busy day times.

Stars

Can you please tell me why do stars glow?

Thank you from Kristina

You know why the Sun shines. Remember the little atomic nuclei banging into each other and giving out energy (p. 13)? Well, it is the same with stars; they too are powered by nuclear energy. In fact, stars are suns. Each star is about as big and powerful as our Sun. I know they don't look it. That's because they are so far away. Recall the electric fire that represented the Sun, you lying on the sofa one metre from the fire representing the Earth, and poor Pluto 40 metres down the road? Well, on that scale, the nearest star would be 250 kilometres away! No wonder they look tiny.

I was lying in bed and
I got out of bed and looked
out of the window and I thought
Why do the **Stars** come out
at night.

Yours Sincerely
Sarah Jarvis (age 9½)

Actually the stars are up there shining down on us *all the time* – day as well as night. The reason we can't see them in the day time is because they are so faint (being so far away from us). We get blinded by all that bright light coming from the Sun and reflecting off the air and dust that make up our atmosphere.

It is only when the Sun sets that we begin to notice the stars. First we see one or two – the brightest of them. Then, as it gets darker, and our eyes get used to the dark, we begin to notice the fainter ones. I know it looks as though more and more of the stars are being 'switched on'. But that is not what is happening; they're 'on' all the time.

I was lying in bed counting sheep trying to get to sleep but I couldn't, I tried and tried but I couldn't So I opened the curtains and started counting stars when I got to 396 it hit me how many stars are there in the world?

yours sincerely
Andrew Metcalfe
age 9

396? Well done! How did you make sure you didn't count the same ones twice? I wonder.

Anyway, as you probably guessed, there are a lot more stars than that. On a clear night, with good eyesight, you might hope to be able to see about 6,000. But that's just a start. If you get hold of a telescope and you point it to a patch of sky where you think there are only a few stars, you will be amazed at what you can see: lots and lots of stars. The extra ones are so far away, they are too faint to see with the naked eye. Not enough light can get through the small 'window' in your eye – what we call the *pupil* of the eye (the black disc at the centre). But a telescope can collect a lot more light than that with its big lens or mirror. That's why the fainter stars can be seen through a telescope. And the bigger the telescope, the *more* stars you can see, as it picks up even fainter light from stars even further away.

It is the same all over the sky. There are masses and masses of faint stars everywhere. It is especially so in the Milky Way. This is a spread-out band of light that stretches from one horizon, right across the sky overhead, to the opposite horizon. You can only see it on very dark clear nights, and if you are away from street lights. If you live in a town, where there is a lot of light reflected from street lights, you might have difficulty noticing it at all. It is called the Milky Way because that is what it looks like; it looks as though the milkman has had an accident and splashed very thin (probably skimmed) milk across the sky.

What actually is it? Why does it glow faintly? It is chock-a-block full of stars – so many stars you can't make them out separately. Their light just adds up to give a general glow.

So, back to your question: How many stars are there?

100,000 MILLION!

Phew! How are we to get our mind round a number *that big*? Well, suppose we decided to give each star a name. That's reasonable, isn't it? After all, our own star has a name: The SUN. What it would mean is that every man, woman and child on Earth would have to think up 20 star names each – none of them being the same. That's how many stars there are!

They are all collected together in a great flat-tened disc – like a CD (only there is nothing compact about *this* disc). It is huge! You remember how we pictured the Earth (you on the sofa) one metre away from the Sun (the electric fire), and how, on that scale, the nearest star was 250 kilometres away? Well, I want you now to think of that 250 kilometres squashed down so that the nearest star is only one metre from the Sun. On that new scale, the *furthest* star in the disc would be 25 kilometres away!

The disc is called the Galaxy. Our Sun is about two-thirds of the way out from the centre of the Galaxy. When we look up at the Milky Way, we are looking towards the centre of the Galaxy; we are looking at the disc of the Galaxy end-on. That's why there are so many stars in that direction.

So, there are a lot of stars. But I haven't finished yet. Read on ...

how many galaxies are there?

age 8 my name
yasseen

I was talking of *the* Galaxy. But you are quite right, Yasseen, there is more than one galaxy. Lots of them. It is difficult to know how many because the bigger the telescope, the fainter the galaxies we see as we probe further and further out into space.

But it is thought that there are probably as many galaxies as there are stars in our Galaxy:

100,000 MILLION!

So now we discover that in order to give each *galaxy* a name, every man, woman and child on Earth would have to come up with 20 names – none of them being the same.

And yes, each of those galaxies has about 100,000 million stars.

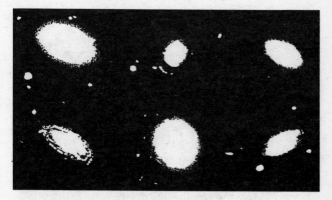

As I said, there are *lots* of stars.

I would love to know the anses of my questin because I find it very intreesting. Hear is my qustien why does the sun not move?

from Abdul (11)

One of the interesting things about being a scientist is when you find out that you've been wrong! At first it was thought that the Earth was flat. But, in fact, it was round. Then it was thought the Earth stood still and the Sun went around it. But that again was wrong – it was the Sun that stood still, and the Earth went around it. The Earth is speeding round the Sun at 30 kilometres per second; that's over 100 times faster than a jumbo jet. (Doesn't feel like it though, does it?)

Now we're wrong again! The Sun *doesn't* stay still. It belongs to the Galaxy, and the Galaxy is rotating; it is spinning slowly about its centre like a giant roundabout. So the Sun is slowly orbiting around the centre of the Galaxy. When I say 'slowly' I mean it takes a long time to get right round – 200 million years to make one complete turn. That's because it has a long way to go. The Sun (and its planets) are actually moving quite fast: 300 kilometres per second around the centre of the Galaxy. That's ten times faster than the Earth's speed in orbit around the Sun. Phew!

And even the centre of the Galaxy doesn't stand still; it is moving at an even greater speed through space: 600 kilometres per second.

I am looking forward to meeting you next month. The questions I will like to ask you are.

1) When there are new Stars What happens to the Old ones.

2) I've Seen a Shooting Star What happens to it When I cant See it anymore

Yours Sincerely

Hannah

age 11

As a star becomes old, it gets to the point where it has just about used up all its fuel. Its nuclear fire is about to go out.

Now, I don't know about you, but I would have thought the star would then quietly fizzle out – like a camp fire dying down when it runs out of wood. But no! We're in for a surprise. In its old age, a star as massive as the Sun cools down all right; it becomes red hot, instead of its usual white hot. But, as I told Ahmad (p. 15), it grows in size. Its fiery gas swells up. One day the Sun will become so large, it will almost swallow up the Earth. At this stage a star is called a *red giant*.

What happens then is that it sheds its outer layers, leaving behind at the centre a small white hot glowing ball. This was the piping hot central core of the star. It is called a *white dwarf*. (Scientists come up with good names, don't you think?) The white dwarf then (at last) quietly fizzles out and becomes cold.

That's for a star like the Sun. Much more massive stars go out with a bang – and I mean that: BANG! One minute they look perfectly normal. Then without any warning, there's a huge explosion. For a short while this one dying star is as bright as all the stars of the galaxy put together. What a way to go!

It's called a *supernova* explosion. As for what's

left over after the explosion, we might find –
close to where the centre of the star was – a *neutron star*. This is a dense ball about 20 kilometres
across. When I say 'dense', I mean a speck of the
stuff, the size of a grain of salt, would weigh the
same as 10,000 crushed up lorries! And neutron
stars spin. How they spin! Some whirl completely around several hundred times a second. We
might not get dizzy on our spinning Earth; but
we certainly wouldn't be able to walk straight
after a ride on a neutron star!

That's one possibility for what you might find
where the old star used to be. Another is even
stranger. Some old stars leave behind a *black hole*.
I'm sure you've heard of those. What happens is
that, while some of the stuff of the star is thrown
out in the supernova explosion, most of it gets
sucked down by its own gravity to a point smaller than the sharp end of a needle. From then on,
anything passing close to this black hole is likely
to get pulled in and squashed down.

Now, you had another question? Ah, yes …
Shooting stars. I love them. Did you know there
are special nights for seeing them – times when
there are likely to be more of them about? If the
sky is clear, I always make a point of going out
to have a look on 10 and 11 December each year.
On those nights, you can generally reckon on

seeing them at the rate of about one a minute. You have to keep your eyes peeled. They shoot across the sky very, very quickly. They come without warning, and you're never sure which part of the sky they will appear in.

The important thing about shooting stars is that they are *not* stars. Although they appear to be about as bright as a star, they are not great balls of fire a long way off in space. Instead, they are small solid particles, generally no bigger than a grain of wheat. They spend thousands of millions of years hurtling about through space until – unlucky for them – they strike the Earth's atmosphere. Then in a matter of a second or two, they burn up. It is this fiery trail that makes up the shooting star. (Because it is not really a star, scientists prefer to call the trail by a different name: a *meteor*.)

Why do the particles burn? Friction. You know how on a cold day you can warm your hands by rubbing them together? We call it heating by *friction*. Well, when the particle enters the atmosphere, it is travelling fast – tens of kilometres per second. As it rubs against the air, it heats up to the point where it glows brightly, melts and boils away. And that's the end of it.

If the particle is bigger, its core might manage to reach the Earth's surface before it has all boiled away. We call such rocks from space *meteorites*.

10
I am 9
bo yirse old   I am in class 1
6 I wold like to know
how meny spase aliens are
theve   and were do thay
live love fvom Lauva
XXX

One thing is for sure: there are no space aliens
living on the other eight planets going around
the Sun. The Earth is the only place that is at the
right kind of temperature. The others are either
too close or too far from the Sun.

But, of course, there are lots and lots of other
suns or stars. LOTS! They were formed in the
same way as the Sun – through a cloud of dust
and gas squashing down under gravity. Many of
these will have planets going around them – for
the same reason as our Sun has planets. Again,
most of these will be too hot or too cold – but
some will be just right. There are surely many

Earthlike planets out there in space – perhaps billions and billions of them. We can't be *absolutely* sure until we've seen them, of course. But that is our best guess to date.

Will they have life on them? We know a lot about how life evolved here on Earth, but not enough to know whether, given the right conditions, it was *bound* to happen. It might have been one big fluke. If it was a lucky fluke, then we humans here on Earth might be the only intelligent form of life in the whole Universe. But I think that's being a bit big-headed. Along with many other scientists I put my money on there being vast numbers of intelligent space aliens out there.

If so, have any of them visited us here on Earth? Despite all talk of UFOs, I reckon it's unlikely. The distance between an alien's sun and our Sun is so great it would stretch space technology to the limit – and frankly I don't think they'd bother. After all, if their technology is *that* good, they can probably pick up our radio and TV transmissions. Now, I ask you: Do you honestly think that an alien tuning into one of our typical chat shows is going to think, 'Gosh, what wise, clever and interesting people. It would be worth travelling 40 million million kilometres to have an intelligent conversation like that'?

The Beginning of the World

Hello my name
is krystle Lakee you may
rember me from my letter that
I wrote to you before
Because you are very braney
Person I am going to ask
quistions about Space and People.
How did the story get around
about the big bang and who
told the story was it a girl,
boy, man, woman? Thank you
for reading my letter

Best wishes
krystle
Lakee.
(Age 11)

There's something very odd about the other
galaxies. They are all moving *away* from each
other. An American astronomer, Edwin Hubble,
noticed that the further away a galaxy was, the
faster it was rushing off into the distance. Carry
on like this and they'll all be gone!

Why are they rushing apart? Because the
Universe started squashed up together, and then
suddenly EXPLODED. The fastest stuff coming

out travels the furthest distance. And that's exactly what we see. The explosion is called the Big Bang.

But how can we be *sure* there was a Big Bang? If we are right, then the Bang must have been very violent. Violent explosions are hot; they give out a lot of heat and light – as happens when a bomb goes off. The flash of light from the Big Bang should still be around in the Universe today – somewhere. There's no other place for it to go! All right, it will have cooled down a long time ago; you wouldn't expect to be able to see it with your eyes any more. These days it would be more like radio waves, or the waves they use in microwave ovens. You can't see those either. But with the right equipment (a Walkman?) you can detect invisible radio waves.

Two other American scientists, Arnold Penzias and Robert Wilson, became the first to discover the radiation from the Big Bang. It is coming down to us out of the sky all the time, day and night. It causes interference on television. If your TV set isn't tuned in properly to the station, you get interference – the picture looks like a snow-storm. Well, about one out of every hundred of those 'snowflakes' is due to the flash of light from the Big Bang. Quite a thought, eh? You didn't know you had a Big Bang detector right in your home, did you!

So that's how the idea of the Big Bang got around.

please can you answer this question
What started the big bang?
from Christopher Moore

We haven't a clue. Why? Because the density of matter in the early universe was so enormous. Today, if we could smear out all the matter to fill up the whole of space, it wouldn't amount to anything more than a very, very thin gas. Now imagine us going back in time, further and further – towards the moment of the Big Bang. The gas gets thicker and denser. It becomes as dense as water, then as dense as rock, then as dense as lead, and so on. In the end, when we get right back, all the way to the very moment of the Big Bang, the density would become MEGA COLOSSAL – it would become infinite. (Infinity is the biggest number anyone can ever think of, multiplied by umpteen zillions, and then you add on a few squillions for luck.) Infinite density is something we scientists cannot handle. And when you grow up and it's *your* turn to be the scientist, I don't see how *you*, or anyone else, is *ever* going to get round this problem.

We're stumped!

I don't know if you will know this question but it's worth a try, here goes,

Do you know how old is the universe is? Please Please try to awnser back because I have been wondering for ages hope you do well on all of Your books

Lot's of

        Love

            Rosie Bunker
            Age 9.

✡

Yes, Rosie, it *was* worth a try because I *do* know the answer – at least I know the rough answer. It is

15,000 million years!

'How can he possibly know that?! Where are the witnesses?' I hear you ask. No, there were no witnesses. Human beings came on the scene for the first time only a few million years ago. (It's funny how in this sort of work you get to thinking that a few million years is '*only*' a few million years.) So, why do we think this?

The galaxies today are still flying apart because of the Big Bang. The further away they are, the faster they are going. If a galaxy is five times further away than another, it will be travelling five times as fast; 20 times further away, 20 times as fast; etc. Now, you don't have to be a genius to work out from this that if we imagine going *back* in time, a point will be reached when all the galaxies were together at the same place. Not only that, knowing how fast the galaxies are moving, and how far they have to go to get on top of each other, you can work out *how long all this takes*. That in turn tells you *when* the Big Bang happened, i.e. 15,000 million years ago. So, that's how we work out the age of the Universe – assuming it was created at the moment of the Big Bang.

I am writing
to tell you how intrested I am
in Science So can you
please answer this question.
Where is the centre of
the universe.
from Christopher Moore
(Age 10)

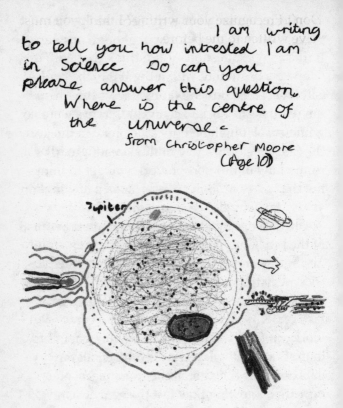

96.

Don't I recognize your writing? I think you must have written to me before.

It's a good question. You'd think that with the Universe beginning with a Big Bang, the explosion must have taken place somewhere. There ought to be a spot you can visit that has a notice saying 'The Big Bang took place here in the year 15,000 million BC.' Alongside there ought to be a souvenir shop – and a café.

In fact, the Big Bang is much more interesting and mysterious than that. It was no ordinary explosion – not the sort where a bomb goes off at one particular point, throwing its debris out into the surrounding space. With *that* kind of explosion you *can* pinpoint where the bomb must have been originally.

The Big Bang was a special kind of explosion – the only one of its kind. At the time of the Big Bang, not only was all of the matter of the Universe squashed down to a point, but *all of space was squashed down to a point too*. There was no space outside the Big Bang. This means we have to think of the Big Bang happening *everywhere*. It is because the Big Bang happened absolutely everywhere, when space was squashed very tiny, you can't think of a particular point being the centre of the Universe – a point where the Big Bang happened and from which all the galaxies are now rushing away.

Just like you, I need help when trying to wrap my mind round these difficult ideas. What I do is this: I imagine a balloon. It starts off very tiny.

But then, as it is blown up, it gets bigger …

and bigger.

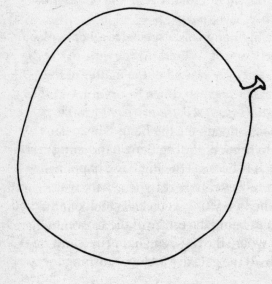

If two flies land on the balloon, they find that they get further and further apart. It is not that they are walking away from each other; they move apart because the rubber in between them is expanding.

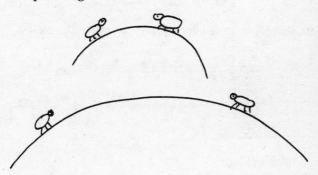

It's the same with the galaxies; the distance between them increases, not because they are moving through space, but because the space between them grows, and as it grows, it carries the galaxies along with it. Space continues to grow today, as it has done ever since the moment of the Big Bang.

Just as you can't look at the surface of the balloon and pick out one particular point from which all the rubber expanded ('the centre of the balloon's surface'), so you can't look at the Universe and pick out any special point where all of space started to expand ('the centre of the Universe').

Scientists say that the world was created by a big bang in the solar system, but in the Bible it says that, God created the world in seven days. Which is true?

Yours Sincerely Oliver Pine
Age 10½

First, let me point out that the Big Bang didn't just happen in the Solar System. The Solar System is the name we give to the Sun and the planets that go round it. As we now know, this is just a very tiny corner of the Universe, no more special than any other part of the Universe. The Big Bang happened everywhere, as I was telling Christopher just now.

But what then of the Bible?

If you go into a library, you will find all sorts of books: children's stories, thrillers, crime, horror, history, poetry, dictionaries, travel books, science books, etc. It's important to know which kind of book you have chosen. It would be silly to read a horror story as though it were history, or a poetry book as though it were science.

So, before starting to read the Bible, you have to ask what kind of book it is. In fact, it is not a book – it is a *collection* of books – a whole library of different kinds of books. And *none* of them are science books! (People were just not very interested in science in those days.)

When it says God created the world in seven days, the important thing is not the 'seven days' bit, but the fact that *God* created the world; he created the Universe and everything in it – including ourselves. So you and I would not exist without God; we owe everything to him. And that means we should be grateful to him, and live our life as he wants us to live it. That's what the Bible is about – not about *how* he actually made the world. For *that* we have to turn to science.

All of this, of course, assumes that there *is* a God. I think there is, but there are others who think not. You will have to make up your own mind about *that*!

I am very intrested in ~~space~~ and would like to know if there are lots of other universes or is there only our universe.

yours

sinserly

Fatima Meho (11)

It's difficult to say. For a start, it depends on what you mean by the word 'universe'.

With more and more powerful telescopes we can see fainter and fainter galaxies; this means we can look further and deeper into space. But there is a limit to how far we can look. The reason has to do with the fact that it takes time for light to travel from one place to another. It takes eight minutes for light to get from the Sun to Earth; it takes four years to get here from the nearest star. What is the maximum time light can take to reach us? Answer: The age of the Universe. Obviously it couldn't have been travelling for longer than that. So, we cannot expect to receive light today that has been travelling for longer than 15,000 million years. That in its turn means that it could not have come from a distance greater than that which light can cover during such a time. We cannot know of the existence of anything that lies further than that. Everything that is *within* that distance, and from which we *could* receive light, is said to be part of 'the observable Universe'.

But we think more than *that* exists. Why? Well, as time goes by, we receive light from further and further away; this is because it has had a longer time to travel. The observable Universe takes in more and more of what lies *outside* it. So, we can say that as well as our observable Universe, there is the rest of the Universe outside – further off into space.

But that still leaves the question of whether there are universes that have their *own* spaces and times – spaces and times that are not part of ours. We just don't know. Indeed, we shall *never* know. If they are not part of our time and space it is impossible to see how we could ever get any messages from them – how we could ever make contact with them. And without that, we can never get proof that they exist.

Abraham   God

The End of the World

I was outside with My friends. I looked around. And thought is it true the world will Came to a end in the year 2,000. And what would happen. would Someone be a lige to tel the story to other people. And how would the world end. Thankyou for taking you time Reading this letter I will Look for would to geting you letter

yours

Sinlerly

Jemma Lamb (Age 10)

People have been predicting when the end of the world will happen for a very long time. They especially like to pick on dates that sound rather special (like the year 2000). Then each time one of these dates comes round, newspapers run scare stories, nervous people hold their breath and, lo and behold, surprise themselves by waking up alive next morning! Then comes the next prediction, and the next, and the next …

If I were you, I wouldn't lose any sleep over the year 2000, or any other year. Keep planning for the future!

I *have* seen your handwriting before! You are always writing to me, Christopher. You are either a budding genius, a nuisance, or a very worried little boy. Why not go and play a bit of football some time?

Anyway, there's no doubt your questions are good ones. You ask: How's the world going to end? As long as you don't get the idea that it's going to happen soon (e.g. the year 2000!), here's what we think:

All the galaxies are flying apart because of the Big Bang. But every galaxy is pulling on every other galaxy with its gravity. So that means the galaxies are gradually slowing down. If they keep this up, they will eventually come to a halt; the expansion of the Universe will be over.

What will happen then? Well, the galaxies can't just sit there in space doing nothing. The gravity between them is still pulling on them. So, from now on, the galaxies start *coming together*. Instead of expanding, the Universe now starts to shrink. This carries on until all the galaxies come piling in on top of each other. We call this a Big

Crunch …

KERPOW!

End of Universe.

So is that how the Universe is going to end? Possibly. It depends on how strong the gravity forces are. After all, as the Universe expands and the galaxies get further apart, the force between them gets weaker. It could be that the force vanishes more or less to nothing before it has managed to stop the galaxies in their tracks; the galaxies will then be able to get clean away; the expansion will go on forever.

What will happen then? The stars will gradually use up all their fuel; their fires will go out. As I was telling Hannah (p. 83) some stars end up as burnt-out cinders, others as cold neutron stars; others as black holes. In between these, there will be a cold gas which gradually thins out as it disappears off into space. Life on all planets will come to an end. And that will be that. We call it The Heat Death of the Universe.

Shiver …
Shiver …
Shiver …
Shiver …

OK, what's it to be: Big Crunch or Heat Death?

Frankly, we don't know. It all depends on the strength of the gravity force. Is it, or is it not, powerful enough to stop the expansion? To answer that, we must know how much matter there is in the Universe, because it's matter that causes gravity. Obviously, the more stuff there is in the Universe, the more gravity. So, how much stuff *is* there? There's no problem adding up the matter in the stars – that's easy. The trouble is: what about all the stuff out there that we *can't* see – because it isn't glowing? We call it *dark matter* – for obvious reasons. And there seems to be an awful lot of it: at least ten times as much as there is matter in the stars and planets – perhaps 100 times as much. We simply don't know as yet. That is one of the first things boys and girls in school today have to find out when they become the scientists of the future.

If I were a betting man, my money, and that of most scientists, would be on the Heat Death. But whether it's to be a Heat Death or a Big Crunch, for goodness' sake don't lose any sleep over it. It's not going to happen for a very … very … very long time.

God

I am a Hindu. In our religion
we have lots of Gods. But my
question is, how many Gods
are there in the whole wrold?
From
Heena
X

Long ago, just about everyone worshipped lots
of gods. Then the idea began to form that there
was in fact only one God. That is what Jews,
Muslims and Christians believe today. Being a
Christian myself, that's what I believe too.

I don't know a great deal about Hinduism, but
I do know you see things rather differently; as
you say, Hindus believe in lots of gods. The trouble with gods (or God) is that they are invisible.
We can't line them up to be counted! So it is not
going to be easy to decide who is right.

But perhaps it doesn't matter all that much?
Surely the important thing is that we both agree
that a God, or gods, exist, and that this affects
the way we should live our lives. For example,

God gave me my life and I am grateful to him for it; you are grateful to one of your gods for the same reason. I show my gratitude by loving God and trying to live my life the way he wants me to live it; you have to love your gods and live your life in a way that pleases them. My God knows me personally, and loves me; the same is true of you and your gods. My God teaches me to love other people; you learn the same from your gods. My God teaches me it is wrong to steal, to kill, to tell lies, to be jealous, to be proud, and so on; you learn much the same things from your gods. My God has promised me that there will be another life for me after my death, and the kind of life it will be depends on how I have lived this life on Earth; you have been told to expect another life too, and that it matters how you have lived this one.

These are the things that *really* matter. Though we have our differences, I think we are both in touch with whatever it is that lies beyond this earthly existence.

Of course, being a Christian myself, I can't help wanting everyone to get to know Jesus. But the people I do worry about are not good Hindus like yourself, but those who don't know any god at all.

I was sunbathing one sunny afternoon, looking up at the sky when I suddenly thought "Whats to stop god falling on top of me?!" I mean if I fell out of a plane without a parachute, I wouldn't just float"!

from Rosy Murray
(Age 11)

What a strange idea! Parachutes?! For a start, I don't see the Man in the Moon wearing a parachute; do I take it you duck every time you see the Moon up there?

When we talk of God as being 'up there' in Heaven, or of Jesus 'ascending into Heaven', we don't mean he is actually up there beyond the clouds; it's just a way of talking. It's like someone getting a big pay rise at work, going out and buying a Porsche car, and a posh house; we say 'He's going up in the world.' But that doesn't mean he has gone to live on a mountain. If you do well in a school test, you 'go to the top of the class'; but that doesn't, of course, mean you now float up to the classroom ceiling.

We have to stop thinking of God sitting on a cloud. He is up there with the clouds all right, but he is also down here – and everywhere else too. He can't fall to Earth, because he's already here – if you see what I mean.

I have a question for you, "when god dies who will be the next god?"

"I hope you can tell me"

Lots of Love
from Hannah (Age 8)

It's true God is the ruler of the world, which makes him a kind of king. And with normal kings, they die and someone else takes over. But with God it's different. He's never going to die. That doesn't mean he just keeps on living and getting old and wrinkled, then very old and very wrinkled, then incredibly old and incredibly wrinkled, then mega old … etc. He doesn't get old at all, and he never gets any wrinkles at all. God never changes – not ever! That's why he will never die.

Don't ask me how he does it. How should *I* know? He's GOD! What he has said is that once we have finished our normal lives here on Earth, he's going to let some of us in on the secret – so that should be good.

Please can
you answer my question ~~you~~
why did God make other
countries.

From Laura Kidridge
age 9

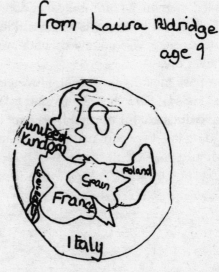

Now, I ask you: What kind of question is *that*?!
I've had some smashing holidays abroad. Not
only that, I've worked in laboratories in the
USA, Italy and Switzerland, and learned a lot
from scientists there. I think the idea of other
countries is great.

Mind you, I simply cannot manage foreign
languages. I do wish only one language had
been invented – English, of course. You'd never
believe just how *terrible* I was at languages when
I was at school; I simply could not remember
what the words meant. In fact, I have a very bad
memory – I can't remember a thing. Very upset-
ting it can be. Except when it comes to watching
films. I enjoy films three times as much as anyone else. How? Because I can watch and enjoy a
film three times before it begins to dawn on me
that I might have seen it before!

I would like to know who am I and what am I?

Yours Sincerely,
Rebecca
7yrs

Phew! That is the BIG question. Some people spend all their lives trying to answer that one, and never doing it. Others never seem to give it a thought. I'm glad you have begun thinking about such things while young. It is important to decide for yourself what you think is the best answer. How you live your life will depend on that answer.

Let's begin with the simpler part of the question: _What_ am I?

There are different ways of tackling it. You might, for example, ask what science has to say about you. I could then describe you as a wonderful, complicated set of atoms. Your brain is a powerful computer; your eye is constructed like an expensive camera; your ear is a highly sensitive microphone; your body has a thermostat for keeping your temperature accurately constant; your heart is a pump that is so reliable it can run for 70 years without a service; you have an immune system for defending you against invasion by all manner of harmful bugs and viruses; when damaged your body can repair itself, etc.

What a truly wonderful object you are! What a pity we can so easily take our bodies for granted.

But then we go on. Scientists say that we human beings are descended from the same ancestors as the apes. It has all happened through a process called Evolution by Natural Selection. In other words, we are a kind of animal. Some people find this a bit shocking. They like to think that there is a big difference between a human and an animal. Personally it doesn't bother me in the slightest. It's another way of answering our question: What am I? I am an animal – but a very special, intelligent animal.

And still we go on. When we look up at night and see the stars, we know that each one of the stars is a sun. They are huge. And there are so many of them. Small wonder the Universe makes us feel small. The movements of the stars and planets would not be affected if you or I never existed. So, from that point of view, we are not important. 'Chemical scum on the surface of a minor planet' is how one scientist has described us. And, in a sense, he is right. That is another way of answering our question – a way that makes us feel very *un*important.

But now we come to something very mysterious about us. We have minds. At this moment, you have thoughts and feelings; you might be happy or sad; you can be kind, angry, loving, hateful, impatient; you can decide where you are going and what you will do next. *The Sun can't do any of these.* It just has to keep moving along in space as it slowly orbits the centre of the Galaxy, dragging its planets along with it – and it doesn't even know it's doing it. Why? Because it doesn't have a mind. It must be *awful* not to have a mind, don't you think? Fancy not knowing anything about what's going on. Fancy not even knowing that you exist. Doesn't this tell you something about the importance of being *you* rather than the Sun?

When we talk about the mind, we have begun to think of that other part of your question: *Who am I?*

When I think of myself, it's mostly that I am thinking of myself as a thinking, feeling person – rather than simply a body. If I were to go deaf or blind, or lose an arm or a leg in an accident, it would still be ME. The same would be true if I had a heart transplant, or if I had a kidney replaced by someone else's. In fact, I could have just about everything changed in my body (except for my brain, which has a lot to do with my mind) and I would still think it was the same me; it would be me with a new body – not me (the body) with a new mind.

Now that's as far as many people go in answering the question: who am I? They simply settle for: a person – one who lives for a while here on Earth, and then dies. They feel free to live their life any way they choose. And when they die, that's the end of them.

Religious people, like myself, see things differently. We believe that there is a God (or gods). God has created us for a purpose. Our lives are not our own to do what we like with. We are to love God, and show that love in the way we behave towards other people. He has taught us to call him 'Father'. He is our Heavenly Father. So that is another way – and I think the most important way – of answering the question: *Who am I?* We are sons and daughters of God.

Flying

Please can you tell me how do airoplanes FLY in the SKY?

From Adil age 7

First of all an aeroplane needs an engine. It sucks in air at the front, and throws it out at the back. In this way, the aeroplane is able to grab hold of the air, and 'pull' itself along.

So far, so good. But all that does is get us rushing down the runway; we're not off the ground yet. How does that happen? That's where the wings come in. The air pushes up on the underside of the wing, and that's what lifts the aeroplane into the sky.

But why does the air do that? Why does it push upwards and not downwards (or no-wards at all)? The answer lies in the cunning shape of the wing. If you look at the aeroplane sideways on, you might be able to see that the wing is curved: it's rounded on top, and flatter underneath. In fact, the pilot is able to change the shape of the wing by moving some loose bits at the back called 'flaps'. When these are pushed out they hang down and so make the shape of the wing hollow underneath. The effect of this is that as the aeroplane moves forward, the air above the wing fairly shoots past the rounded top surface, while that underneath tends to get caught up in the hollow. That way the air underneath the wing builds up and gets denser than that above. So, with more air underneath pushing up on the wing than there is air on top pushing down, the aeroplane rises up into the sky.

That's what they tell me – the aeroplane makers. And I'm sure they're right. It's a very sensible explanation. But I don't know. Every time I see one of those giant metal boxes lumbering down the runway, filled with people, baggage, duty-free booze, plastic meals, toilets, etc., I can't help thinking: This is stupid. It'll *never* make it. How can *air* hold up all that lot? But it does! Weird!

Please can you tell me
Why can't an aeroplane
go in Space? from Daniel age7

The higher up you go, the thinner the air becomes. In the end you run out of air altogether. You are then in *space*.

But an aeroplane needs air to pull itself along with. No air, no aeroplane.

That's why if you want to go into space you have to find some other way of doing it – a rocket. A rocket is a bit like a flying gun. With a gun, as the bullet comes shooting out of the end, the gun itself jerks in the opposite direction. The gun pushes the bullet forward, but the bullet also pushes the gun backwards. We say the gun 'recoils'. Of course, the gun doesn't come flying back into your hand at the same speed as the bullet goes forward – just as well! That's because it's heavier than the bullet.

The same sort of thing happens in a rocket. What happens is that the rocket engine heats up some gas, and then throws it out. It pushes on the gas, and the gas pushes back on the rocket. The rocket 'recoils' in the opposite direction from that of the gas. So, if the gas goes shooting off to the rear; the rocket moves off in the forward direction. The gases are much lighter than the rocket (just as the bullet was lighter than the gun), so the gases have to come out very fast (they have to be hot) in order to push back hard enough on the heavy rocket to get it moving.

In this way, a rocket doesn't need to be in air. It carries its own supply of gases to push on.

I am dreming about my DaD and my mum hoding hands.

Mind and Dreams

I would like it if you could answer the question

When people are thinking about something, how do they forget it? Where does it go in your mind? ? ? ??

yours
sincerely,
Priscilla
aged 11yrs

Your mind is a fascinating mystery. Nobody really understands it. The mind is all to do with thinking. At this very minute you are thinking about these words you are reading, and you are having feelings such as being chilly, hungry, bored, tired, etc. Those thoughts are going on in your mind.

But there is more to the mind than that. For example, while you were reading that last sentence you were not thinking about the date of your birthday. But if I were now to ask you, 'When is your birthday?' you would be able to tell me immediately; you would not have to go and look up your birth certificate to find out. So that information must have been in your mind all along – even when you weren't actually thinking about it. And not only your birth date but a whole heap of other knowledge – all that stuff you've learned at school and hope to be able to churn out when you sit a test or exam.

That's why it is helpful to imagine the mind to be divided up into two parts: the *conscious* part (where you do your thinking and feeling) and the *unconscious* part. When we say a boxer has been knocked 'unconscious', we mean he is lying on the floor not thinking of anything. But once he has recovered, he will start thinking again (and probably feeling a headache). Well, there is a part of your mind that is unconscious. And that is where you store all the information in your memory. It waits there until the conscious part of your mind needs it.

You have two kinds of memory: short-term and long-term memories. So, for example, if I ask you what you had for breakfast this morning you probably could tell me. But if I ask you in ten years' time what you had for breakfast today you would reckon I was mad thinking you'd be able to remember a thing like that. That is because some sorts of information only go into your short-term memory. Remembering what you had for breakfast this morning could be useful to your parents later in the day if they want to know whether you finished off the cereal packet; they would then know whether to buy some more. But that sort of information won't be useful in 10 years' time, so it never gets put into your long-term memory. Instead, after a short while, it gets wiped.

As I was telling Laura just now, I have a terrible memory. I keep on forgetting people's names. Very embarrassing it can be. As for that game Trivial Pursuit, I *hate* it. I try to convince myself I wouldn't want my mind filled up with all that rubbishy useless kind of information, anyway. But I guess that's just sour grapes.

Please why do we see colours?
Do we see colours like other
people?

from Ashkan Sawhani

Light behaves like a wave. It moves about
through space like ripples spreading out over the
surface of a pond. With ripples on a pond, the
humps and dips can either be squashed tightly
together, or they can be stretched out. The same
is true of light waves. The humps and dips of
light waves can either be squashed up close to
each other, or more spread out. And that is what
makes the difference between light of different
colours; it's all due to the distance between the
humps and between the dips. We call it the
'wavelength' of the light. Different wavelengths
belong to different colours. Red light has the
longest wavelength, then comes orange, yellow,
green, blue, indigo and finally violet. White light
is a mixture of *all* these colours – the colours of
the rainbow (which is odd because we usually
think that white isn't coloured at all). Red light
has about twice the wavelength of violet light.

So far so good. That was me – as a scientist –
talking about light. But that's not what you

wanted to know. You wanted to know why it is that when light of a particular wavelength enters your eye, what you see (in your mind) is that particular colour.

Frankly, I haven't a clue. Nobody does. (Why do kids ask such *impossible* questions?!) It is one of those great mysteries of the mind.

As for whether I see in my mind the same colour as you do in yours – when we look at the same light – there seems no way of finding out. I can only know *my* mind; you can only know *yours*. I suspect we might *not* see the same thing. After all, some people are colour blind – they can't tell the difference between certain colours, where we would think the difference was obvious. I can only think they must be seeing something different from us.

The fact that we each have our own favourite colours might also mean that we see things differently. I have a granddaughter who can't stand brown; I like it, and she claims I *always* wear brown clothes. Sometimes when I am visiting her I deliberately choose non-brown clothes and shoes; I know the first thing Melanie will do when she sees me is inspect my clothes for anything brown. And blow me, no matter how hard I try, she always finds there's a bit of it somewhere!

I would be grateful if you could answer my question but if not it doesn't matter.

I would like to know how people's minds work? Like some people love robbing and mugging people. Some seem so kind and gentle they don't seem human! Why are our personalities like this?

Hope to see you soon
age 10
love Sara Whines

There are various possible reasons.

Firstly, there is the way a person has been brought up. What kind of home did they come from? What sort of school did they go to? If, when you are young, you are surrounded by people who are well-behaved, thoughtful and kind, then you will grow up thinking that that is *normal* behaviour. That must increase the chances that you will also act like that. If, on the other hand, you were always being knocked about by a selfish bully of a father, you will probably grow up thinking that getting your own way by hitting others is the normal way to behave.

But that isn't the whole story. You probably know some pretty dreadful kids at school who come from perfectly good homes; others you can really make good friends with, even though they have to put up with all kinds of trouble at home. This brings us to another reason for our behaviour: we are *born* different. Two children brought up in the same home with the same parents, going to the same school, can turn out differently.

When we look at animals, we find that they tend to behave in certain ways *from birth*. No one has to teach a cat how to hunt; right from birth it knows how to do it. The same seems to be true of us; some of us, from birth, tend to act in certain ways, others in different ways.

What you are born with, and how you are brought up, both have an effect on the sort of person you turn out to be. Which is the more important of the two? No one really knows.

But one thing is certain: there is a *third* way in which our behaviour is affected. Quite simply, people can *decide* how they are going to behave. Each of us has a choice. It doesn't matter how rotten your home might be, or how bad tempered you might be born, with enough guts you can *make* yourself into the kind of person you want to be. I suggest you decide which kind of person you want to be – and then you go for it!

Why do people go mad?.

I hope you can answer my question

Yours
Sincerely

Elizabeth. C.
Age 11 yrs.

That's a very difficult one. For a start, it is not always clear which people are mad and which are normal. By 'normal' we mean people who think more or less like most other people. But to some extent we all think differently – and a good thing too. It would be very boring if we all thought the same. If we didn't have some people who saw the world very differently from the rest of us, there would be no scientific geniuses like my hero, Einstein.

But how different do you have to be before you get called 'mad'? It's hard to say. Certainly if someone is living a miserable life and threatening to kill themselves, or they are seeing things that are not really there, or hearing imaginary voices, or they are always imagining that everyone is out to get them, or they're so confused that they can't look after themselves – then they need help.

Luckily, there is a lot that can be done for such people today: there are medicines and there are doctors who help patients to talk through their problems and see things differently.

Some people are born mentally ill. This must be because there is something not quite right with their brain from the very beginning. Others seem normal to begin with, but then become mentally ill later on. It is hard to say why this happens. It might be because the mix of chemicals in their brain goes a bit haywire. That's when medicines can help; they can change the mix and get it back to normal.

With some people their brain simply wears down in old age and they can no longer think as clearly as they used to. This happens to all of us to some extent; it just happens faster for some people.

Mental illness must be an awful thing to have to put up with. I think I would rather have almost any other kind of illness than a mental one.

Perhaps we can all do our little bit to help such people by not calling them 'mad'. If we say someone is 'mad', it's as though we are saying they are a different kind of person from ourselves. They are not – any more than someone who is ill with flu is a different kind of person. They are simply ill, and we must be helpful and thoughtful towards them like we would be to anyone who was suffering from any other kind of illness.

when I go to sleep I have a dreams I would like to know why do we have dreams?

from Abdul

Dreams seem to come from the unconscious part of our mind.

Remember how I was telling Priscilla (p. 133) about the unconscious? I said that it was where our memories are stored. But we mustn't think the unconscious just sits there doing nothing. It isn't like a dusty old library where the books of information simply wait on the shelves until someone (the conscious part of the mind) comes along and picks them up. There is a lot going on in the unconscious mind all the time.

For example, I was saying how I find it difficult to remember names. Often it's on the tip of my tongue, but no matter how hard I try, it just won't come. So, what do I do? I get on with something completely different. And then, perhaps after half an hour, I get to thinking about that person again and, lo and behold, the name is there this time! No trouble at all. It is there just waiting for me to ask! How did this happen?

I don't know for sure, but it seems like this: while my conscious mind was getting on with something else, the unconscious part was busily sifting through the memories to find the name I wanted. By the time my conscious mind asked the question a second time, the unconscious part was ready with the answer.

Another way the unconscious works is this. You might dislike something – such as going into the water at the seaside. You don't understand why you feel that way; everybody else seems to enjoy it. Well, it's possible you had a frightening experience when you were little. Perhaps you were at a swimming bath. Someone was mucking around and held your head down under the water rather a long time. At the time it scared you. But you soon forgot about it. At least your *conscious* mind forgot it, but your unconscious didn't. Now, every time you get close to a lot of water, the unconscious part of your mind gets worried. Remembering what happened that other time, it warns the conscious part by sending danger signals. So without you really understanding why, you shy away from going into the sea. That, then, is another way your unconscious can affect you.

Getting back to dreams. When you are awake, all sorts of sounds and sights are coming at you all the time, demanding your attention. At night time, when you are asleep, it's quite different. With everything quiet, this is a good time for the unconscious to send its own messages into the conscious part of your mind. If, for example, you've got an exam coming up at school, you might be worrying about it – deep down. At night, thoughts about having to go through some kind of test are likely to come into your mind. When this happens, you start dreaming. If your unconscious is frightened about something, it will send you frightening thoughts – and this is what we call a nightmare.

It can be quite fascinating trying to work out what the unconscious is trying to say through dreams. But my guess is that most of the time it just sends up a lot of rubbish not worth bothering about. It is only when you keep getting the same sort of dream, night after night, that you perhaps ought to take it seriously.

thank you for coming to
are class and Talking ta us about the
world I like to talk about Dreams.
Can you answer my question?
Do are dreams tell us more then we
think and Do are dreams tell us
something in the future

your sincerly

Leonard
Lewis

I was telling Abdullah just now that our dreams
come from the unconscious. For that reason you
would expect them to be able to tell us something about what was going on in that part of
our mind – the part that is usually hidden from

us. But it is not as simple as that. Important messages from the unconscious often get mixed up with other thoughts that seem to be just plain silly. It can be quite hard deciding what the dreams are really trying to tell us. It might take an expert to sort it out (the experts are called 'psychiatrists'). But yes, our dreams can tell us something about ourselves.

As for your other question: can dreams tell us about the future? There are some stories in the Bible about people who seem to have had a look into the future through their dreams. And we have all heard of people today who have strange stories to tell: 'I dreamed last night that I got a letter from my long-lost aunt in Australia. And guess what, next morning I woke up and there was a letter from her!' Do such stories *prove* that dreams can tell us about the future? We have to be careful. What about all the times we have dreams and what we dream about does *not* happen? After all, no one would be so boring as to go around saying, 'I dreamed last night that I got a letter from my long-lost aunt in Australia. And guess what, next morning I woke up and there still wasn't any letter from her!'

I'm sorry to be a spoilsport, but I don't see how dreams *can* really tell us about the future. But who knows, one day I might be in for a shock!

Growing Up and Getting Old

I am in year 6 and would like to know how come I am geting old and old? please tell me.
From
Rachel Potter
age 10
help me

Oh dear! Are you worrying about that already?!

At first, growing old is fun. It's something to look forward to. As each year goes by you get bigger and stronger. You can do things you couldn't do when you were little. Bullies at school now think twice before picking on you. You go from being a child to an adult. You discover that you are in charge of a wonderful body – a machine that is far, far more marvellous than any machine we scientists can ever put together.

But then in your late teens and early twenties, things start to change. Your body, like any other body that has to keep going non-stop, starts to show the first signs of wear. Perhaps your eyesight begins to get worse; or you don't hear as well as you used to; later, your knees start to creak and it becomes uncomfortable to walk; or you notice that when you cut yourself, it takes longer to heal.

No one likes these sorts of changes. Luckily there is often something that can be done about them. For example, I now wear glasses to read, and I have a hearing aid. With these I am able to carry on much the same as I have always done.

Getting old is nothing to be frightened of. It happens to us all. The only way *not* to grow old is to die young – and who wants to do *that*?!

There is a saying: 'You are as old as you think you are.' I think that's very true. I sometimes think that, in my mind, I never really grew up completely. I feel a bit like a boy wearing a grown-up's body, pretending to be grown up.

There's something special about being old; you have memories to look back on. You know more than you ever did before. You have learned so much from experience. I used to look forward to being 50. 'I will be at my best when I am 50', I used to say. I was wrong. I am at my best *now* – when I am 63 – and it's getting better all the time. I can honestly say that I am happier now than I have ever been, and I wouldn't swap with anyone younger.

One evening when
I went to see a cousin
his mum said that I had
grown so much the almost
couldnt recognise me. After
she had said that I started
to think about how bones
grew with our bodies.
  could you tell me how
bones grow?

Yours sincerely
Daniel Towers

(Age 10)

I'm afraid I don't know very much about this. I never studied biology at school. But I showed your letter to a friend of mine who is a biology teacher. What she told me was that a bone, like the long bones in your legs, grows at two places. These are 'bone-making factories'. (She didn't actually use those words – she used big biology-type words I can never remember.) These 'factories' are close to each end of the bone.

Bone, like everything else in your body, is made up of round cells. You can think of cells as another kind of Lego block. Cells sometimes split in two. Each half then settles down to being round, and grows to the same size as the first cell. So now you have two cells instead of one. These then split to give four cells, the four become eight, and so on. That is what happens in the 'bone-making factories'. More and more cells are made, and this gives more and more bony stuff. That way, the bone grows, you get taller, and your cousin's mum gets amazed when she sees you.

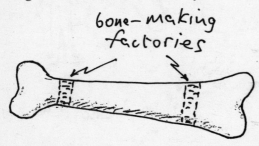

bone-making factories

I was lying in bed thinking about my family. Then I came up with this question. Why do children grow and then when they become grown-ups they stop growing?
Aslo why can't we see people growing?
I hope you can answer my questions.

Yours

Sincerely

Helen Anderson. (Age 10.)

I'll start with your second question – it's easier!

The reason we can't see ourselves growing is that we grow so slowly. It's the same with the hands of a clock. If you watch the hands, they don't seem to be moving. It's only when you go off and do something else, and then come back to take a look, that you can see a change. That's how it is with children growing.

As for what *stops* you growing. It's all to do with the many changes going on in your body as you go from being a girl to being a woman. Your body makes juices called 'hormones'. And these go around the body at that time making changes so as to get you ready for having babies. In particular, the hormones recognize that you are big enough by now to have babies, so the bone-making factories can be shut down; you don't need to be made any bigger. (In any case, who wants to be a giant?)

Mind you, the body is very clever. Although it shuts down these factories, it still has ways of making new bony stuff as and when it's needed. So, if you have an accident and break a leg, new bony stuff can be made to patch up the break.

Lucky Dip

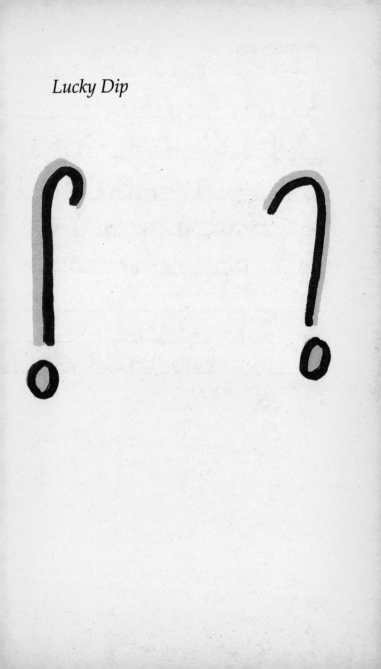

I have some questions
for you how is
electricity made people
can't just make
it and it dosen't
just apear from nowear

Yours sincerly
Caroline Alkinson

No it doesn't come from nowhere. I explained to Lin (p. 3) about atoms: how there was a nucleus at the centre of the atom and tiny electrons buzz-ing around the outside. What I didn't tell Lin was *why* the electrons stick closely to their nucleus.

The answer is this: both the nucleus and the electrons carry something called 'electric charge'. It comes in two kinds: positive charge on the nucleus, and negative charge on the electrons.

Positive and negative charges pull on each other; they like to get together. It's the electric force from the nucleus that stops the electrons from wandering off. It's a bit like the way the gravity force of the Sun stops the Earth drifting off into space.

If an atom is on its own, the electrons are held quite tightly to their nucleus by this force between their electric charges. But when atoms are squashed close together (as they usually are) the electrons can get a little confused. They are still being pulled by their nucleus, but they are also being pulled by the nuclei belonging to neigh-bouring atoms. The outer electrons of certain kinds of atom can come loose; they are not sure which atom they belong to any more. They wan-der from one atom to another. This happens, for example, to the copper atoms of a copper wire.

And that's how we get electricity. When you switch on an electric light, the loose electrons get pulled through the wires. Because each electron carries electric charge, there is a flow of electric charge. That is what we mean by an 'electric current'. It's like the flow of water in a river. We call that a current too.

It's hard work pushing the electrons round the wires. That's the job of power stations. They get the energy they need for this from burning coal, oil or gas – or they might use nuclear power. Sometimes power stations can use water. If water collects in a lake high up in the mountains, it can be let out gradually and falls down pipes due to gravity. Its energy at the bottom of the mountain can then be used to push the electrons along.

But that's all very well, you might say. Electricity is a flow of electric charge. But what exactly *is* electric charge? That is a question we cannot answer – and what's more, I reckon no one is *ever* going to answer it. In science all we can say is how things *behave*, not what things *are*. So, we can say that if things have electric charge, they can pull and push each other around. That way we can understand how things move about. But what electric charge actually *is*, remains a mystery.

Where does lightning come from?
I hope you can answer

From Rachel Hopkinson
Age 7

Lightning happens when there are thick dark clouds about. Clouds are made of water droplets and tiny pieces of ice. As these move about, they rub against each other and some of the electrons get separated from their nuclei. The nuclei are swept upwards on the tiny ice crystals, while the knocked-off electrons hitch a ride on the downward falling droplets. So there is a build-up of positive electric charge high up in the clouds, and of negative electric charge at the bottom of the clouds.

This cannot go on for ever. As you know, there is a pulling force between positive and negative electric charges. The electrons at the bottom of the cloud pull on the nuclei that have now been taken to the top of the cloud. Not only that, they pull on the nuclei of the atoms belonging to the ground. As the charges build-up, these forces get stronger and stronger. In the end, something has to give. Like a shot, the electrons and their separated nuclei suddenly rush back together again. Either that, or the electrons and the nuclei of the atoms of the ground make a dash to join up. And that is what we mean by lightning. It is the sudden surge of electric current in the air.

In this rush, the electrons bang into atoms along the way. Some of their energy gets changed into the energy of light. And that's what gives the jagged white line you see in the sky. It marks the path taken by the electric current. You can see it clearly as a line when the lightning strikes the ground – what we call *forked* lightning. If the lightning is between the bottom and the top of the clouds it will be hidden from us by the cloud. In that case, the lightning lights up the whole cloud; that's what we call *sheet* lightning.

Lightning strikes more than 100 times per second, every second, somewhere on Earth.

I think there is nothing more thrilling than watching a really good thunderstorm. (Though, to be honest, they still scare me rigid – even when I watch them from the safety of indoors!)

> *I would like to now how police dogs can find people who are breaking the law?*
>
> *Yours sincerely*
> *Harriet Cook*
> *7yrs*

First of all, let me say that dogs aren't clever enough to be able to look at a person and decide 'That's a criminal if ever I saw one' – if that's what you meant by your question!

The thing about dogs is that they have very good noses; they can pick up smells that are too faint for us to notice. So, the police sometimes take a dog to the scene of a crime in the hope that it might pick up the scent of the criminal. Each of us pongs a bit – some more than others! If the criminal has left something behind, perhaps a glove, or a knife, or has been handling things like the door knob with a sweaty hand, then he will leave a trace of smell behind. The dog takes a good sniff and remembers that smell. Apparently, to a dog we all smell differently. It can then follow the trail of smell left behind by the criminal as he made his escape. And with luck, the dog can track him down.

One day I was in
my room listening to Criss Cross
when all of a sudden a thought struck
me. Why do we have sound?
I tried and tried to think why, but I
could'nt think why, but I could'nt

yours sincerely

Stewart Chromik.

Suppose you are playing a CD, what happens is
this: the middle part of the loudspeaker is made
to vibrate back and forth. The higher the note
being played, the *faster* the vibrations. The louder
the note being played, the *bigger* the vibrations.

This vibrating loudspeaker pushes against the
layer of air next to it, squashing it. This squashed
layer of air now pushes on the next layer,

squashing that one. This then pushes on the next … etc. This carries on across the room.

In the end, it's the layer of air next to the middle part of your ear that is being pushed. This part of your ear is called your 'ear drum'. In this way your ear drum is set vibrating. It is now vibrating in the same way as the loudspeaker was. When this happens, you hear a sound in your mind – the music being played by the CD. (Don't ask me why. No one knows why vibrating an ear drum should match up with a sound heard in your mind. It just does. Put it down to another of life's mysteries.)

And that goes for all sounds – not just those produced by loudspeakers. Whenever something makes a sound it disturbs the air, and this disturbance travels through the air and sets your ear drum vibrating.

You have to be careful not to listen to sounds that are too loud. They will set your ear drum vibrating so hard it might split, and that will damage your hearing. I have a son who plays in a pop group. (They are called Big Audio. Ever heard of them? They're very popular in the USA.) About once a year he persuades me to go along to one of their gigs. I get worried when I notice that the sound is so loud my chest is vibrating in time with the music. I now always take cotton wool with me. Much better, and safer that way!

I would like to know how we know if the refridgerator light is off once we have closed the door.

Yours sincerely,
Simon Holder
8yrs

What a suspicious mind you have!

Normally you have to push a switch to turn a light off. With a fridge, the light switch is placed so that it is pushed by the door as it closes. So, when you close the door, the door can't help but push the switch, and so turn the light off for you. That's the idea – and I myself am happy to believe that the light really does go out.

But if you are still not sure, you could try peeking through the crack of the door just as it closes; you might see it go out. One thing I would warn you *not* to do: DON'T unload the fridge and sit in it to see what happens. You might get stuck in there – and boy, will you be in trouble when you come out!

Fobbing Off!

I was on a plane to France when I said to my Dad "where is the end of the world?" Dad said "I don't know only experts know!"

The next day we went to a zop we looked at lots of animals then I asked to my Dad "how many animals are there in the world?" Dad said "I don't know only experts know." That night I asked my older sister Angela If there is going to be another world after this one? Angela said "I don't know go to sleep."

The next morning I asked Dad the same question Dad said "I don't know!" have you packed your bag?"

I hope you can help me with these questions!

        Yours sincerely

Sarah Wilson   10 years old

As you have probably guessed, you are being fobbed off. Parents and older brothers and sisters get like that. They never answer questions properly; they're so busy doing their own thing, they keep putting you off. Let's see if I can help:

Where is the end of the world? That depends on what you mean by 'world'. If you mean the Earth, then it doesn't have an end. When people thought the Earth was flat, they did worry about where this flat Earth ended – after all, they didn't want to fall over the edge! But now we know it's round, not flat. That means we can carry on forever; we never come to an end because we keep coming back to our starting point.

Perhaps, on the other hand, when you spoke of 'the world', you meant 'the Universe'. In that case it is hard to say where it ends – even for the 'experts'! The problem is that the Universe takes in everything – including space. If we came to the edge of the Universe, then beyond that edge there would be nothing – in other words, empty space. But space, even if it's empty, is part of the Universe. So that means we have *not* got to the end yet! Do you see what I'm getting at?

To get round this problem, the experts say that there cannot be an edge. No matter how far you travel, there will still be more of the Universe ahead of you. The Universe will be infinite.

It's either that, or you get back to where you

started. That's a funny thought, isn't it? You start your space journey in a certain direction, and you carry on and on, keeping to a straight line. Then blow me, before you know it, you land back where you started! (It's a bit like someone going right the way round the Earth, without knowing it was actually round.)

Your second question: How many animals?

I've no idea. Nobody has counted them. But it's a lot. If you did count them you would end up with one of those huge squillion-type numbers. It would be a number so big you wouldn't be able to take in what it really meant anyway. So, what's the point? If you want to count them, that's OK by me. But leave me out. (Oh dear, that's sounds like a fob-off!)

Finally: Another world after this one?

I take it you're asking whether there will be another sort of life after this one. From the very earliest days, people, wherever they lived, were sure that this life was not the only one. We can tell that from the way people in olden days buried their dead. They were often buried with things they would be needing for their journey to another life.

Today many people believe the same thing. Some of us, for example, believe we shall go to a different life with God. Hindus believe you come back to this life in another form. Either way, the kind of life you have beyond death depends on how you have lived this life.

Not everyone agrees with this. There are many people who think that when you die, that is the end of you.

It is not for me to tell you what to think. This is something where experts are of no use. You have to make up your own mind. All I will say is that it is important that you *do* make up your mind; don't let it just drag on and on. That's because what you think happens after death affects everything you should be doing in *this* life. You don't want to live your life only to discover at the end of it that you got it all wrong!

Just Before I Go …

Do you by any chance have the same problem as Sarah in that last letter? Do your parents fob you off when you ask questions?

If so, help is at hand! Why don't you send your big Earth-shattering question to Uncle Albert? See if you can mind-boggle *him*. It can be a question about anything you like – as long as it is a really BIG QUESTION. Send it to:

Uncle Albert's Post Bag
c/o Faber and Faber
3 Queen Square
London WC1N 3AU

Write neatly. You can include a drawing, if you like. And who knows? Your letter might appear in the next book in the series of *Letters to Uncle Albert*.

Until next time
Lots of love

Russell Stannard
(aged 63)

The Children

Abdullah (11)
Mark Walton
Ben (9)
Manprit Gill (10)
Paul
John
John Baldry (11)
David
Fatima Meho (11)
Andrew Buchanan
Sarah
Adam Chandler
Saira Soarez (11)
Kathyrn Brown (9)
Melissa Benfell (10)
Melanie (10)
David Debney (9)
Thomas Compton
Elliot Wright (9)
Sophie Fowler
Mark Currie (11)
Hugo (8)
Laura Bishop
Matthew (5)
Kyle (9)

Kristina
Yasseen (8)
Hannah (11)
Laura (6)
Luke
Maxime Patall
Christopher Moore (10)
Ben Ashton (9)
Abraham
Jemma Lamb (10)
Abdulah
Rosy Murray (11)
Hannah (8)
Laura Aldridge (9)
Katie Foster (10)
Alex Piatti (11)
Adil (7)
Daniel (7)
Sandra
Rashmi
David Nicholls
Danielle Kingsley (9)
Leonard Lewis
Caroline Atkinson
Stewart Chromik (10)
Matthew Parting (10)
Sarah Wilson (10)
Sarah Jarvis (9½)
Andrew Metcalfe (9)

Simon Holder (8)
Harriet Cook (7)
Rachel Hopkinson (7)
Helen Anderson (10)
Daniel Towers (10)
Rachel Potter (10)
Elixabeth C (11)
Krystle Lakee (11)
Lin (8)
Ahmed (10)
Emma
Joseph Stewart (9)
Sarah Bartholomew
Naomi Durston
Rosie Bunker (9)
Oliver Pine (10½)
Heena
Rebecca (7)
Priscilla (11)
Ashkan Sawhani
Sara Whines (10)
Steven Jones (10)
Stephanie Orme (9)
Hal Jarrett
Jamie Oilk